Survey of Law School Faculty 2025, Evaluating the Law School Curriculum

AF680662

 ISBN 979-8-88517-294-3

Table of contents

THE QUESTIONNAIRE

1. Please give us the following contact information:

   A. Name:
   B. Organization:
   C. Title
   D. Email address:

2. You are:

   A. Professor
   B. Assistant/Associate Professor
   C. Lecturer or Research Fellow
   D. Adjunct/Clinical Faculty
   E. Emeritus
   F. Other (please specify)

3. How old are you?

   A. Under 30
   B. 30-39
   C. 40-49
   D. 50-59
   E. 60 or Over

4. Are you male or female?

   A. Male
   B. Female
   C. Transgender

5. Your law school has approximately how many students?

6. Is your law school public or private?

   A. Public
   B. Private

7. In the past semester how many courses did you teach?

   A. None
   B. One
   C. Two
   D. More than Two

8. Which phrase best approximates the view of your law school taken by organizations that rank law schools?

A. Top 20 law school
B. Somewhere in the 21-75 rank
C. 76 to 250
D. Other

9. Which phrase best characterizes your political beliefs?

A. Right of Conservative
B. Conservative
C. Centrist
D. Liberal
E. Left of Liberal
F. Curriculum Development

10. The curriculum at your law school should emphasize practical legal skills more. To what degree do you agree or disagree?

A. Strongly agree
B. Agree
C. Neither agree nor disagree
D. Disagree
E. Strongly disagree

11. Your law school should lower tuition or increase student aid for students who commit to pursue public interest or legal aid legal services for a specified period after graduation. Do you agree or disagree?

A. Strongly agree
B. Agree
C. Neither agree nor disagree
D. Disagree
E. Strongly disagree

12. Your laws school more than adequately prepares its students to learn about and deploy new technologies important in legal services. Do you agree or disagree?

A. Strongly agree
B. Agree
C. Neither agree nor disagree
D. Disagree
E. Strongly disagree

13. How confident are you in the effectiveness of 2-year rather than the traditional 3-year legal education programs?

A. Extremely confident
B. Very confident
C. Somewhat confident
D. Not so confident
E. Not at all confident

14. Law students in your program should spend less time in class and more time in internships, legal aid clinics, and other real world experience. Do you agree or disagree?

A. Strongly agree
B. Agree
C. Neither agree nor disagree
D. Disagree
E. Strongly disagree

15. How would you change your law school's curriculum if given the opportunity?

16. How difficult is it at your institution to develop new law courses in emerging or neglected areas?

A. Very easy
B. Easy
C. Neither easy nor difficult
D. Difficult
E. Very difficult

Characteristics of the sample

Academic title

	#
Professor	61
Assistant/Associate Professor	21
Adjunct/Clinical Faculty	28
Emeritus	15
Other	9
Total	134

Age of respondent

	#
Under 40	6
40-49	19
50-59	33
60 or over	75
Unknown	1
Total	134

Gender of respondent

	#
Male	80
Female	50
Other	4
Total	134

Public or private law school

	#
Public	81
Private	53
Total	134

# of courses taught las semester

	#
None	27
One	40
Two	59
More than two	8
Total	134

Approximate Self Assessed Law School Ranking

	#
Top 20 law school	27
Somewhere in the 21-75 rank	55
76 to 250	46
Other	6
Total	134

Political views

	#
Conservative	14
Centrist	34
Liberal	65
Left of Liberal	20
Unknown	1
Total	134

Law school enrollment

	#
Less than 400	32
400+ - 550	32
550+ - 800	34
More than 800	36
Total	134

INSTITUTIONAL AFFILIATIONS OF THE SURVEY PARTICIPANTS

IU McKinney
Belmont University College of Law
Benjamin N. Cardozo School of Law
Bennett Law Firm
Boston University School of Law
BU School of Law
Buffalo State University
Cardozo
Carey Law, U Maryland
Charleston School of Law
Chicago-Kent
Columbia Law School
Creighton University School of Law
Duke Law
Emory University
Fisher Broyles
Fordham Law School
Fordham University School of Law
Harvard Law School
Howard University
Indiana University
LMU Law School
LMU Loyola Law School
Louisiana State Univ. Law Center
LSU Law Center Juvenile Defense Clinic
LSU Law, Tulane law
Marquette University Law School
MC Law
McGill University
Mercer Univ. School of Law
Mississippi Supreme Court
Mitchell Hamline School of Law
MSU College of Law
New England Law | Boston
Northeastern University School of Law
Northern Illinois University College of Law
Northwestern Law School
OU Law
Pace Law School
Pepperdine Caruso Law
Public Counsel
Roger Williams University School of Law
Rutgers Law School
Salesforce, Inc.
Santa Clara University School of Law
Schulich School of Law
SMU Law School

Southern University Law Center
St. Mary's University School of Law
Stetson University College of Law
Temple Law School
The Ohio State University Moritz College of Law
The University of Tennessee College of Law
Thomas Jefferson School of Law
Thurgood Marshall S of Law
UCI law
UCLA School of Law
UGA School of Law
UIC Law
UMass Law School
UMKC Law School
UNC-CH
Univ. of Washington School of Law
University of Arkansas
University of California Irvine Law School
University of California San Francisco law
University of Connecticut Law School
University of Florida
University of Georgia Law School
University of Idaho
University of Illinois Chicago Law School
University of Iowa, College of Law
University of Maryland School of Law
University of Mississippi, School of Law
University of Nebraska - Lincoln College of Law
University of North Carolina School of Law
University of Oklahoma College of Law
University of Oregon School of Law
University of Richmond
University of South Dakota Law School
University of St. Thomas -- Minnesota
University of Tennessee
University of Texas
University of Toronto
University of Tulsa
University of Virginia
University of Wyoming
UT Law and Bush School
UVA Law
UW School of Law
Villanova University
Washington Univ in St Louis
Wayne State University Law School
William S. Boyd School of Law, UNLV
Wise Law Library, CU Boulder
Yale Law School

SUMMARY OF MAIN FINDINGS

The survey assessed faculty opinions on law school curriculum development, focusing on practical legal skills, tuition policies, technology training, experiential learning, course development, and alternative legal education models.

View of the Importance of Emphasis on Practical Legal Skills

We asked: . The curriculum at your law school should emphasize practical legal skills more. To what degree do you agree or disagree?

F. Strongly agree
G. Agree
H. Neither agree nor disagree
I. Disagree
J. Strongly disagree

- 51.49% of faculty agreed or strongly agreed that law school curricula should emphasize practical legal skills more, while 22.39% disagreed or strongly disagreed.
- Assistant/Associate Professors (61.91%) and Adjunct/Clinical Faculty (67.86%) were the strongest supporters.
- Professors (44.26%) and emeritus faculty (20.00%) were more skeptical.
- Faculty at public law schools (50.61%) were more supportive than those at private schools (52.83%).
- Younger faculty (<50 years old) were the strongest supporters, while those 60+ were less enthusiastic.

Views on the Advisability of Tuition Reductions for Public Interest Commitment

We asked: . Your law school should lower tuition or increase student aid for students who commit to pursue public interest or legal aid legal services for a specified period after graduation. Do you agree or disagree?

Strongly agree
Agree
Neither agree nor disagree
Disagree
Strongly disagree

- 63.43% of faculty supported tuition reductions or increased aid for students who commit to public interest legal work post-graduation.
- Professors (67.21%) showed the highest agreement, while adjunct/clinical faculty (64.29%) were slightly less supportive.

- Faculty at schools with 550-800 students (74.53%) showed the highest support, while smaller schools (<400 students) were least supportive (46.88%).
- Political divide was evident, with liberals (72.31%) and left-of-liberals (60.00%) strongly supporting, while conservatives (14.29%) showed minimal support.

Law Schools' Current Capabilities in Preparing Students in Legal Technology

We asked: Your laws school more than adequately prepares its students to learn about and deploy new technologies important in legal services. Do you agree or disagree?

A. Strongly agree
B. Agree
C. Neither agree nor disagree
D. Disagree
E. Strongly disagree

- 47.02% agreed that law schools prepare students well for legal technology, but 23.88% disagreed.
- Adjunct/Clinical Faculty (67.86%) were the most positive, while Emeritus Faculty (40.00%) were more skeptical.
- Private law schools (34.53% agreement) were perceived as lagging compared to public institutions (55.55%).
- Younger faculty (<50) were more optimistic about tech training compared to older faculty.

Support for Two-Year Rather than Three-Year Legal Education

We asked: How confident are you in the effectiveness of 2-year rather than the traditional 3-year legal education programs?

A. Extremely Confident
B. Very Confident
C. Somewhat Confident
D. Not so Confident
E. Not at All Confident

- 75.37% of faculty were not confident in two-year legal education models.
- Professors were the most resistant (74.41% not confident), while Adjunct/Clinical Faculty (71.43%) were slightly more open to the idea.
- Confidence was highest among younger faculty (33.33% somewhat confident under 40), while older faculty (>60) showed the least confidence (5.33% extremely or very confident).

Value of Legal Experiential Learning vs. Traditional Classroom Time

We asked: Law students in your program should spend less time in class and more time in internships, legal aid clinics, and other real world experience. Do you agree or disagree?

A. Strongly agree
B. Agree
C. Neither agree nor disagree
D. Disagree
E. Strongly disagree

- 29.85% supported reducing classroom time in favor of internships and legal clinics, while 45.52% disagreed.
- Adjunct/Clinical Faculty (57.14%) were the strongest supporters, while Professors (55.73%) were the most opposed.
- Top 20 law school faculty (37.04%) were more supportive compared to faculty at lower-ranked schools.
- Political divide: Liberals (29.23% agree) and conservatives (35.71% disagree) differed in views.

Challenges in Developing New Courses

We asked: How difficult is it at your institution to develop new law courses in emerging or neglected areas?

A. Very easy
B. Easy
C. Neither easy nor difficult
D. Difficult
E. Very difficult

- 51.50% found course development "Easy" or "Very Easy," while 14.18% found it difficult.
- Emeritus faculty found it easiest (73.33%), while Assistant/Associate Professors (19.05% found it difficult) faced the most hurdles.
- Larger institutions (800+ enrollment) were more flexible, with 66.66% finding it easy, compared to smaller schools.

Breakout Analyses with Greatest Explanatory Power

- Faculty Rank: Adjunct/Clinical Faculty strongly support practical skills and experiential learning, while Professors are more traditionalist.
- Institution Size: Larger law schools are more open to tuition aid for public interest careers and technology training.

- Political Views: Conservatives resist tuition incentives for public interest and experiential learning, while liberals are more supportive.
- Age: Younger faculty (<50) support practical skills, experiential learning, and tech training more than older faculty.

How Should Law School Curriculum Change?

The responses reflect diverse opinions, with some advocating for greater practical skills training and others emphasizing traditional legal education.

Theme	Key Responses
More Experiential Learning	"Require at least one semester of externships," "More clinical opportunities," "Mandatory law clinics for all students"
Emphasis on Technology	"Add AI training in legal practice," "Expand legal research tech courses," "More coursework on digital evidence and e-discovery"
More Writing & Research	"Increase legal writing in upper-level courses," "Integrate writing into doctrinal classes," "Require 3 years of legal writing instead of 1"
Balancing Theory & Practice	"Law school should be more like medical school—first two years doctrinal, third year clinical," "Less focus on theoretical courses, more on real-world practice"
Reducing Cost & Barriers	"Lower tuition for students pursuing public interest," "Expand financial aid for students from underrepresented communities"
More Flexible Course Offerings	"Offer more elective courses in specialized fields," "Give students greater freedom in choosing their coursework"
Dissatisfaction with Current Model	"Law school is too expensive and does not prepare students for real legal work," "Too many vanity courses that do not benefit students"
Opposition to Change	"The current curriculum is fine," "Less emphasis on clinical work, more on fundamental legal principles"

Conclusions

- Most faculty support practical skills but are divided on how much to integrate into the curriculum.
- There is strong support for tuition incentives for public interest careers.
- Law schools are seen as needing improvement in legal technology training.
- Most faculty oppose two-year legal education models.
- Experiential learning is a contested issue, with adjunct faculty favoring it and professors resisting major shifts.
- Larger law schools are more open to curricular flexibility than smaller institutions.

Table 1.1 The curriculum at your law school should emphasize practical legal skills more. To what degree do you agree or disagree?

	Strongly agree	Agree	Neither agree nor disagree	Disagree	Strongly disagree
Entire sample	26.12%	25.37%	26.12%	18.66%	3.73%

Table 1.2 The curriculum at your law school should emphasize practical legal skills more. To what degree do you agree or disagree? Broken out by law school enrollment

Law school enrollment	Strongly agree	Agree	Neither agree nor disagree	Disagree	Strongly disagree
Less than 400	25.00%	31.25%	21.88%	18.75%	3.13%
400+ - 550	25.00%	18.75%	34.38%	18.75%	3.13%
550+ - 800	32.35%	11.76%	32.35%	20.59%	2.94%
More than 800	22.22%	38.89%	16.67%	16.67%	5.56%

Table 1.3 The curriculum at your law school should emphasize practical legal skills more. To what degree do you agree or disagree? Broken out by academic title

Academic title	Strongly agree	Agree	Neither agree nor disagree	Disagree	Strongly disagree
Professor	19.67%	27.87%	24.59%	24.59%	3.28%
Assistant/Associate Professor	38.10%	23.81%	33.33%	4.76%	0.00%
Adjunct/Clinical Faculty	39.29%	28.57%	10.71%	14.29%	7.14%
Emeritus	13.33%	20.00%	46.67%	13.33%	6.67%
Other	22.22%	11.11%	33.33%	33.33%	0.00%

Table 1.4 The curriculum at your law school should emphasize practical legal skills more. To what degree do you agree or disagree? Broken out by age of respondent

Age of respondent	Strongly agree	Agree	Neither agree nor disagree	Disagree	Strongly disagree
Under 40	33.33%	33.33%	33.33%	0.00%	0.00%
40-49	36.84%	36.84%	10.53%	15.79%	0.00%
50-59	27.27%	33.33%	30.30%	9.09%	0.00%
60 or over	21.33%	18.67%	28.00%	25.33%	6.67%
Unknown	100.00%	0.00%	0.00%	0.00%	0.00%

Table 1.5 The curriculum at your law school should emphasize practical legal skills more. To what degree do you agree or disagree? Broken out by gender of respondent

Gender of respondent	Strongly agree	Agree	Neither agree nor disagree	Disagree	Strongly disagree
Male	22.50%	21.25%	28.75%	22.50%	5.00%
Female	32.00%	30.00%	24.00%	14.00%	0.00%
Other	25.00%	50.00%	0.00%	0.00%	25.00%

Table 1.6 The curriculum at your law school should emphasize practical legal skills more. To what degree do you agree or disagree? Broken out by public or private law school

Public or private law school	Strongly agree	Agree	Neither agree nor disagree	Disagree	Strongly disagree
Public	30.86%	19.75%	28.40%	19.75%	1.23%
Private	18.87%	33.96%	22.64%	16.98%	7.55%

Table 1.7 The curriculum at your law school should emphasize practical legal skills more. To what degree do you agree or disagree? Broken out by # of courses taught last semester

# of courses taught last semester	Strongly agree	Agree	Neither agree nor disagree	Disagree	Strongly disagree
None	25.93%	22.22%	33.33%	14.81%	3.70%
One	30.00%	32.50%	15.00%	20.00%	2.50%
Two	25.42%	20.34%	28.81%	22.03%	3.39%
More than two	12.50%	37.50%	37.50%	0.00%	12.50%

Table 1.8 The curriculum at your law school should emphasize practical legal skills more. To what degree do you agree or disagree? Broken out by ranking

Ranking	Strongly agree	Agree	Neither agree nor disagree	Disagree	Strongly disagree
Top 20 law school	22.22%	22.22%	25.93%	14.81%	14.81%
Somewhere in the 21-75 rank	29.09%	20.00%	29.09%	20.00%	1.82%
76 to 250	23.91%	32.61%	21.74%	21.74%	0.00%
Other	33.33%	33.33%	33.33%	0.00%	0.00%

Table 1.9 The curriculum at your law school should emphasize practical legal skills more. To what degree do you agree or disagree? Broken out by political views

Political views	Strongly agree	Agree	Neither agree nor disagree	Disagree	Strongly disagree
Conservative	28.57%	14.29%	14.29%	42.86%	0.00%
Centrist	23.53%	23.53%	26.47%	23.53%	2.94%
Liberal	27.69%	30.77%	26.15%	12.31%	3.08%
Left of Liberal	25.00%	15.00%	35.00%	15.00%	10.00%
Unknown	0.00%	100.00%	0.00%	0.00%	0.00%

Table 2.1 Your law school should lower tuition or increase student aid for students who commit to pursue public interest or legal aid legal services for a specified period after graduation. Do you agree or disagree?

	Strongly agree	Agree	Neither agree nor disagree	Disagree	Strongly disagree
Entire sample	20.15%	43.28%	22.39%	11.19%	2.99%

Table 2.2 Your law school should lower tuition or increase student aid for students who commit to pursue public interest or legal aid legal services for a specified period after graduation. Do you agree or disagree? Broken out by law school enrollment

Law school enrollment	Strongly agree	Agree	Neither agree nor disagree	Disagree	Strongly disagree
Less than 400	12.50%	34.38%	34.38%	15.63%	3.13%
400+ - 550	21.88%	40.63%	28.13%	6.25%	3.13%
550+ - 800	35.29%	38.24%	17.65%	5.88%	2.94%
More than 800	11.11%	58.33%	11.11%	16.67%	2.78%

Table 2.3 Your law school should lower tuition or increase student aid for students who commit to pursue public interest or legal aid legal services for a specified period after graduation. Do you agree or disagree? Broken out by academic title

Academic title	Strongly agree	Agree	Neither agree nor disagree	Disagree	Strongly disagree
Professor	14.75%	52.46%	19.67%	8.20%	4.92%
Assistant/Associate Professor	14.29%	38.10%	33.33%	9.52%	4.76%
Adjunct/Clinical Faculty	21.43%	42.86%	21.43%	14.29%	0.00%
Emeritus	33.33%	33.33%	13.33%	20.00%	0.00%
Other	44.44%	11.11%	33.33%	11.11%	0.00%

Table 2.4 Your law school should lower tuition or increase student aid for students who commit to pursue public interest or legal aid legal services for a specified period after graduation. Do you agree or disagree? Broken out by age of respondent

Age of respondent	Strongly agree	Agree	Neither agree nor disagree	Disagree	Strongly disagree
Under 40	16.67%	66.67%	16.67%	0.00%	0.00%
40-49	21.05%	42.11%	26.32%	5.26%	5.26%
50-59	18.18%	27.27%	42.42%	12.12%	0.00%
60 or over	21.33%	49.33%	13.33%	12.00%	4.00%
Unknown	0.00%	0.00%	0.00%	100.00%	0.00%

Table 2.5 Your law school should lower tuition or increase student aid for students who commit to pursue public interest or legal aid legal services for a specified period after graduation. Do you agree or disagree? Broken out by gender of respondent

Gender of respondent	Strongly agree	Agree	Neither agree nor disagree	Disagree	Strongly disagree
Male	21.25%	43.75%	15.00%	15.00%	5.00%
Female	18.00%	42.00%	36.00%	4.00%	0.00%
Other	25.00%	50.00%	0.00%	25.00%	0.00%

Table 2.6 Your law school should lower tuition or increase student aid for students who commit to pursue public interest or legal aid legal services for a specified period after graduation. Do you agree or disagree? Broken out by public or private law school

Public or private law school	Strongly agree	Agree	Neither agree nor disagree	Disagree	Strongly disagree
Public	19.75%	44.44%	23.46%	11.11%	1.23%
Private	20.75%	41.51%	20.75%	11.32%	5.66%

Table 2.7 Your law school should lower tuition or increase student aid for students who commit to pursue public interest or legal aid legal services for a specified period after graduation. Do you agree or disagree? Broken out by # of courses taught last semester

# of courses taught last semester	Strongly agree	Agree	Neither agree nor disagree	Disagree	Strongly disagree
None	29.63%	37.04%	18.52%	11.11%	3.70%
One	20.00%	42.50%	25.00%	7.50%	5.00%
Two	15.25%	47.46%	22.03%	13.56%	1.69%
More than two	25.00%	37.50%	25.00%	12.50%	0.00%

Table 2.8 Your law school should lower tuition or increase student aid for students who commit to pursue public interest or legal aid legal services for a specified period after graduation. Do you agree or disagree? Broken out by ranking

Ranking	Strongly agree	Agree	Neither agree nor disagree	Disagree	Strongly disagree
Top 20 law school	11.11%	55.56%	11.11%	11.11%	11.11%
Somewhere in the 21-75 rank	25.45%	45.45%	21.82%	5.45%	1.82%
76 to 250	21.74%	32.61%	28.26%	17.39%	0.00%
Other	0.00%	50.00%	33.33%	16.67%	0.00%

Table 2.9 Your law school should lower tuition or increase student aid for students who commit to pursue public interest or legal aid legal services for a specified period after graduation. Do you agree or disagree? Broken out by political views

Political views	Strongly agree	Agree	Neither agree nor disagree	Disagree	Strongly disagree
Conservative	0.00%	14.29%	14.29%	50.00%	21.43%
Centrist	5.88%	61.76%	17.65%	14.71%	0.00%
Liberal	29.23%	43.08%	23.08%	4.62%	0.00%
Left of Liberal	30.00%	30.00%	35.00%	0.00%	5.00%
Unknown	0.00%	100.00%	0.00%	0.00%	0.00%

Table 3.1 Your laws school more than adequately prepares its students to learn about and deploy new technologies important in legal services. Do you agree or disagree?

	No Answer	Strongly agree	Agree	Neither agree nor disagree	Disagree	Strongly disagree
Entire sample	0.75%	8.96%	38.06%	28.36%	19.40%	4.48%

Table 3.2 Your laws school more than adequately prepares its students to learn about and deploy new technologies important in legal services. Do you agree or disagree? Broken out by law school enrollment

Law school enrollment	No Answer	Strongly agree	Agree	Neither agree nor disagree	Disagree	Strongly disagree
Less than 400	0.00%	6.25%	40.63%	28.13%	21.88%	3.13%
400+ - 550	0.00%	6.25%	43.75%	21.88%	25.00%	3.13%
550+ - 800	0.00%	14.71%	41.18%	26.47%	14.71%	2.94%
More than 800	2.78%	8.33%	27.78%	36.11%	16.67%	8.33%

Table 3.3 Your laws school more than adequately prepares its students to learn about and deploy new technologies important in legal services. Do you agree or disagree? Broken out by academic title

Academic title	No Answer	Strongly agree	Agree	Neither agree nor disagree	Disagree	Strongly disagree
Professor	0.00%	6.56%	34.43%	29.51%	22.95%	6.56%
Assistant/ Associate Professor	4.76%	4.76%	33.33%	38.10%	19.05%	0.00%
Adjunct/ Clinical Faculty	0.00%	14.29%	53.57%	14.29%	10.71%	7.14%
Emeritus	0.00%	13.33%	26.67%	40.00%	20.00%	0.00%
Other	0.00%	11.11%	44.44%	22.22%	22.22%	0.00%

Table 3.4 Your laws school more than adequately prepares its students to learn about and deploy new technologies important in legal services. Do you agree or disagree? Broken out by age of respondent

Age of respondent	No Answer	Strongly agree	Agree	Neither agree nor disagree	Disagree	Strongly disagree
Under 40	16.67%	0.00%	33.33%	33.33%	16.67%	0.00%
40-49	0.00%	10.53%	47.37%	31.58%	5.26%	5.26%
50-59	0.00%	9.09%	27.27%	27.27%	27.27%	9.09%
60 or over	0.00%	9.33%	41.33%	28.00%	18.67%	2.67%
Unknown	0.00%	0.00%	0.00%	0.00%	100.00%	0.00%

Table 3.5 Your laws school more than adequately prepares its students to learn about and deploy new technologies important in legal services. Do you agree or disagree? Broken out by gender of respondent

Gender of respondent	No Answer	Strongly agree	Agree	Neither agree nor disagree	Disagree	Strongly disagree
Male	0.00%	7.50%	42.50%	30.00%	17.50%	2.50%
Female	2.00%	10.00%	32.00%	28.00%	22.00%	6.00%
Other	0.00%	25.00%	25.00%	0.00%	25.00%	25.00%

Table 3.6 Your laws school more than adequately prepares its students to learn about and deploy new technologies important in legal services. Do you agree or disagree? Broken out by public or private law school

Public or private law school	No Answer	Strongly agree	Agree	Neither agree nor disagree	Disagree	Strongly disagree
Public	0.00%	11.11%	44.44%	22.22%	19.75%	2.47%
Private	1.89%	5.66%	28.30%	37.74%	18.87%	7.55%

Table 3.7 Your laws school more than adequately prepares its students to learn about and deploy new technologies important in legal services. Do you agree or disagree? Broken out by # of courses taught last semester

# of courses taught last semester	No Answer	Strongly agree	Agree	Neither agree nor disagree	Disagree	Strongly disagree
None	0.00%	14.81%	37.04%	25.93%	18.52%	3.70%
One	0.00%	7.50%	45.00%	25.00%	17.50%	5.00%
Two	1.69%	6.78%	33.90%	32.20%	20.34%	5.08%
More than two	0.00%	12.50%	37.50%	25.00%	25.00%	0.00%

Table 3.8 Your laws school more than adequately prepares its students to learn about and deploy new technologies important in legal services. Do you agree or disagree? Broken out by ranking

Ranking	No Answer	Strongly agree	Agree	Neither agree nor disagree	Disagree	Strongly disagree
Top 20 law school	0.00%	14.81%	40.74%	29.63%	11.11%	3.70%
Somewhere in the 21-75 rank	0.00%	12.73%	47.27%	21.82%	12.73%	5.45%
76 to 250	2.17%	2.17%	28.26%	32.61%	32.61%	2.17%
Other	0.00%	0.00%	16.67%	50.00%	16.67%	16.67%

Table 3.9 Your laws school more than adequately prepares its students to learn about and deploy new technologies important in legal services. Do you agree or disagree? Broken out by political views

Political views	No Answer	Strongly agree	Agree	Neither agree nor disagree	Disagree	Strongly disagree
Conservative	0.00%	7.14%	35.71%	28.57%	28.57%	0.00%
Centrist	0.00%	2.94%	52.94%	23.53%	17.65%	2.94%
Liberal	1.54%	10.77%	32.31%	30.77%	16.92%	7.69%
Left of Liberal	0.00%	15.00%	35.00%	25.00%	25.00%	0.00%
Unknown	0.00%	0.00%	0.00%	100.00%	0.00%	0.00%

Table 4.1 How confident are you in the effectiveness of 2-year rather than the traditional 3-year legal education programs?

	Extremely confident	Very confident	Somewhat confident	Not so confident	Not at all confident
Entire sample	3.73%	5.22%	15.67%	38.06%	37.31%

Table 4.2 How confident are you in the effectiveness of 2-year rather than the traditional 3-year legal education programs? Broken out by law school enrollment

Law school enrollment	Extremely confident	Very confident	Somewhat confident	Not so confident	Not at all confident
Less than 400	3.13%	9.38%	9.38%	34.38%	43.75%
400+ - 550	3.13%	6.25%	18.75%	40.63%	31.25%
550+ - 800	5.88%	0.00%	11.76%	41.18%	41.18%
More than 800	2.78%	5.56%	22.22%	36.11%	33.33%

Table 4.3 How confident are you in the effectiveness of 2-year rather than the traditional 3-year legal education programs? Broken out by academic title

Academic title	Extremely confident	Very confident	Somewhat confident	Not so confident	Not at all confident
Professor	3.28%	4.92%	16.39%	29.51%	45.90%
Assistant/ Associate Professor	0.00%	9.52%	23.81%	38.10%	28.57%
Adjunct/Clinical Faculty	10.71%	7.14%	10.71%	46.43%	25.00%
Emeritus	0.00%	0.00%	13.33%	46.67%	40.00%
Other	0.00%	0.00%	11.11%	55.56%	33.33%

Table 4.4 How confident are you in the effectiveness of 2-year rather than the traditional 3-year legal education programs? Broken out by age of respondent

Age of respondent	Extremely confident	Very confident	Somewhat confident	Not so confident	Not at all confident
Under 40	0.00%	0.00%	33.33%	50.00%	16.67%
40-49	5.26%	0.00%	21.05%	36.84%	36.84%
50-59	0.00%	15.15%	12.12%	48.48%	24.24%
60 or over	5.33%	2.67%	14.67%	33.33%	44.00%
Unknown	0.00%	0.00%	0.00%	0.00%	100.00%

Table 4.5 How confident are you in the effectiveness of 2-year rather than the traditional 3-year legal education programs? Broken out by gender of respondent

Gender of respondent	Extremely confident	Very confident	Somewhat confident	Not so confident	Not at all confident
Male	2.50%	3.75%	17.50%	37.50%	38.75%
Female	2.00%	8.00%	12.00%	42.00%	36.00%
Other	50.00%	0.00%	25.00%	0.00%	25.00%

Table 4.6 How confident are you in the effectiveness of 2-year rather than the traditional 3-year legal education programs? Broken out by public or private law school

Public or private law school	Extremely confident	Very confident	Somewhat confident	Not so confident	Not at all confident
Public	2.47%	6.17%	13.58%	43.21%	34.57%
Private	5.66%	3.77%	18.87%	30.19%	41.51%

Table 4.7 How confident are you in the effectiveness of 2-year rather than the traditional 3-year legal education programs? Broken out by # of courses taught last semester

# of courses taught last semester	Extremely confident	Very confident	Somewhat confident	Not so confident	Not at all confident
None	0.00%	11.11%	22.22%	33.33%	33.33%
One	7.50%	2.50%	10.00%	52.50%	27.50%
Two	0.00%	5.08%	15.25%	33.90%	45.76%
More than two	25.00%	0.00%	25.00%	12.50%	37.50%

Table 4.8 How confident are you in the effectiveness of 2-year rather than the traditional 3-year legal education programs? Broken out by ranking

Ranking	Extremely confident	Very confident	Somewhat confident	Not so confident	Not at all confident
Top 20 law school	3.70%	3.70%	22.22%	40.74%	29.63%
Somewhere in the 21-75 rank	3.64%	3.64%	14.55%	38.18%	40.00%
76 to 250	2.17%	8.70%	10.87%	36.96%	41.30%
Other	16.67%	0.00%	33.33%	33.33%	16.67%

Table 4.9 How confident are you in the effectiveness of 2-year rather than the traditional 3-year legal education programs? Broken out by political views

Political views	Extremely confident	Very confident	Somewhat confident	Not so confident	Not at all confident
Conservative	0.00%	14.29%	35.71%	28.57%	21.43%
Centrist	2.94%	5.88%	17.65%	35.29%	38.24%
Liberal	4.62%	3.08%	12.31%	44.62%	35.38%
Left of Liberal	5.00%	5.00%	10.00%	30.00%	50.00%
Unknown	0.00%	0.00%	0.00%	0.00%	100.00%

Table 5.1 Law students in your program should spend less time in class and more time in internships, legal aid clinics, and other real world experience. Do you agree or disagree?

	Strongly agree	Agree	Neither agree nor disagree	Disagree	Strongly disagree
Entire sample	9.70%	20.15%	24.63%	35.07%	10.45%

Table 5.2 Law students in your program should spend less time in class and more time in internships, legal aid clinics, and other real world experience. Do you agree or disagree? Broken out by law school enrollment

Law school enrollment	Strongly agree	Agree	Neither agree nor disagree	Disagree	Strongly disagree
Less than 400	12.50%	25.00%	25.00%	28.13%	9.38%
400+ - 550	9.38%	21.88%	28.13%	31.25%	9.38%
550+ - 800	8.82%	17.65%	26.47%	41.18%	5.88%
More than 800	8.33%	16.67%	19.44%	38.89%	16.67%

Table 5.3 Law students in your program should spend less time in class and more time in internships, legal aid clinics, and other real world experience. Do you agree or disagree? Broken out by academic title

Academic title	Strongly agree	Agree	Neither agree nor disagree	Disagree	Strongly disagree
Professor	4.92%	14.75%	24.59%	40.98%	14.75%
Assistant/ Associate Professor	0.00%	38.10%	9.52%	42.86%	9.52%
Adjunct/Clinical Faculty	28.57%	28.57%	17.86%	17.86%	7.14%
Emeritus	0.00%	13.33%	40.00%	40.00%	6.67%
Other	22.22%	0.00%	55.56%	22.22%	0.00%

Table 5.4 Law students in your program should spend less time in class and more time in internships, legal aid clinics, and other real world experience. Do you agree or disagree? Broken out by age of respondent

Age of respondent	Strongly agree	Agree	Neither agree nor disagree	Disagree	Strongly disagree
Under 40	0.00%	66.67%	0.00%	16.67%	16.67%
40-49	21.05%	21.05%	10.53%	42.11%	5.26%
50-59	0.00%	33.33%	30.30%	30.30%	6.06%
60 or over	12.00%	10.67%	28.00%	36.00%	13.33%
Unknown	0.00%	0.00%	0.00%	100.00%	0.00%

Table 5.5 Law students in your program should spend less time in class and more time in internships, legal aid clinics, and other real world experience. Do you agree or disagree? Broken out by gender of respondent

Gender of respondent	Strongly agree	Agree	Neither agree nor disagree	Disagree	Strongly disagree
Male	7.50%	18.75%	23.75%	36.25%	13.75%
Female	8.00%	24.00%	28.00%	34.00%	6.00%
Other	75.00%	0.00%	0.00%	25.00%	0.00%

Table 5.6 Law students in your program should spend less time in class and more time in internships, legal aid clinics, and other real world experience. Do you agree or disagree? Broken out by public or private law school

Public or private law school	Strongly agree	Agree	Neither agree nor disagree	Disagree	Strongly disagree
Public	9.88%	22.22%	24.69%	32.10%	11.11%
Private	9.43%	16.98%	24.53%	39.62%	9.43%

Table 5.7 Law students in your program should spend less time in class and more time in internships, legal aid clinics, and other real world experience. Do you agree or disagree? Broken out by # of courses taught last semester

# of courses taught last semester	Strongly agree	Agree	Neither agree nor disagree	Disagree	Strongly disagree
None	11.11%	14.81%	33.33%	29.63%	11.11%
One	17.50%	20.00%	20.00%	35.00%	7.50%
Two	1.69%	20.34%	25.42%	40.68%	11.86%
More than two	25.00%	37.50%	12.50%	12.50%	12.50%

Table 5.8 Law students in your program should spend less time in class and more time in internships, legal aid clinics, and other real world experience. Do you agree or disagree? Broken out by ranking

Ranking	Strongly agree	Agree	Neither agree nor disagree	Disagree	Strongly disagree
Top 20 law school	18.52%	18.52%	22.22%	29.63%	11.11%
Somewhere in the 21-75 rank	9.09%	12.73%	29.09%	38.18%	10.91%
76 to 250	4.35%	26.09%	21.74%	36.96%	10.87%
Other	16.67%	50.00%	16.67%	16.67%	0.00%

Table 5.9 Law students in your program should spend less time in class and more time in internships, legal aid clinics, and other real world experience. Do you agree or disagree? Broken out by political views

Political views	Strongly agree	Agree	Neither agree nor disagree	Disagree	Strongly disagree
Conservative	7.14%	28.57%	0.00%	21.43%	42.86%
Centrist	5.88%	23.53%	20.59%	38.24%	11.76%
Liberal	12.31%	16.92%	35.38%	32.31%	3.08%
Left of Liberal	10.00%	15.00%	15.00%	50.00%	10.00%
Unknown	0.00%	100.00%	0.00%	0.00%	0.00%

How would you change your law school's curriculum if given the opportunity?

Top 20 law school

1 More instruction; less crap.
2 No change
3 Add more experiential learning courses
4 I would make externships mandatory for at least one semester. I would require more practical skills course but perhaps tracked to where students see themselves practicing. Not every student want to be a litigator. Some aspire to be transactional attorneys, others regulatory, and others prefer alternative dispute resolution.
5 More business courses.
6 More writing opportunities
7 Increase number of internship opportunities
8 I would have more courses in law and technology.
9 I would add a leg-reg class to the required curriculum in place of "con law 2"
10 I'd have more moot court experience,
11 It works really well. I would delete the requirement for a second Crim pro or con law class.
12 Spend a day inside a prison after taking criminal law. Spend three days at a school after taking education Law. And so on.
13 Less Clinical, more Academic
14 Increased experiential requirements including a mandatory law clinic
15 Trial Tactics, Appellate argument, Real world candidate current issues
16 More transactional education
17 ADD TECHNOLOGY TRAINING AS A REQUIREMENT

Somewhere in the 21-75 rank

1 I WOULD NOT CHANGE MUCH AND TRY TO BALANCE CONFLICTING VIEWS RATHER THAN CHOOSE STONGLY ON the past. THAT IS BECAUSE FEW ACTIONS BELONG FULLY AND PREDICTABLY TO ONE GROUP, AND NEVER CHANGE. ONE MUST BE AWARE OF THE GROUP, AND NATIONAL CULTURE RATHER THAN BE LINKEDTO ONE. AND one should ADJUST WHEN THE REASONS OF his or her BECOMES MORE IMPORTANT AS THE GROUP'S SITUATIONS AND NATINAL SITUATION CHANGES. I would adjust. AFTER ALL, GROUP Life IS Changeable, as well as the group's members' life and national and international culture and economic and other aspects of life, and knowledge change,
2 I think every student should do a clinic. I think it is so important
3 Increase experiential opportunities; add more clinical programs
4 Provide more courses tailored to those students who are not planning or have no Interest In public interest programs.

5 More practice based courses.
6 Law schools should switch to a model analogous to medicine in which the first two years would be intensive training in: (1) sophisticated legal analysis (not blackletter doctrine)[2) interdisciplinary training in policy and advocacy; and (3) clear, effective, and creative writing. The third year should be spent in supervised internships with feedback and review by clinical faculty.
7 More required courses, more required curves
8 More Family Law
9 I would expand the more academic offerings Roman Law, e.g.
10 Devoted more credits to core subjects and better developing core competencies. Encourage all students to take some experiential credit (clinic, externship, internship, etc.) but not allow them to take up to 1-1/2 full semesters' worth of credits in experiential courses.
11 More AI in the classrooms.
12 More on the business of law, i.e. how to make a living as a lawyer.
13 Make it more skill-focused and practical. Better merge legal skills courses and doctrinal courses.
14 Add to environmental law curriculum
15 More niche courses and more practicums.
16 I would remove the optional "track" so that students are not so constrained in their class choices.
17 Reassess which courses are required
18 More focus on skills and writing.
19 More real world application
20 More rigor-- less clinical--we have too much narrow subject matter clinical education
21 No major changes
22 More interprofessionality; more opportunity for integration/holistic education
23 I would require all full time law faculty to return to practice for a year (every 4 years) so that practice experience would naturally be incorporated into the courses and it would reflect current practice.
24 Require a supervised live client clinic
25 More mandatory public law and international courses
26 Our school does an amazing job of requiring clinical education and having robust externship programs to balance coursework. I think other schools should do the same.
27 Make it more functional and practical. Give students more opportunity to write and receive feedback on their writing.
28 Less identity politics, less feminism, less CRT.
29 Make LRW a full Lawyering skills class Require co-teaching to leverage diverse faculty
30 Assessments in all levels would not be single end of semester exams. The ABA requires professors grade and that has created a one-test model. It's contrary to good pedagogy.
31 I responded "disagree" in response to questions about more practical training, because my school already emphasizes practical training to a high degree. Most of our students engage in a large number of

practicums, externships, and experiential courses. I would change the curriculum by adding a basic legal knowledge and skills course before the 1L fall semester.

32 Less teaching by tenured professors with minimal real-world experience representing clients and more by faculty who have actually practiced as a lawyer and can teach them what it is like to be a practicing lawyer and the skills required for that.

33 Longer semesters

34 More empathy on academic fundamentals such as Tory's, contracts

35 Three year writing program, rather than dropping it after one year. Business Associations not required.

36 Balance doctrinal and skills learning by coordinating courses and clinics; encourage experiential learning

37 More opportunities for faculty-guided experiences in legal practice

38 Fewer theoretical course, fewer clinics, more fundamental courses.

39 More freedom to choose classes

40 Make required courses more uniform

41 More clinical and Moot Court opportunities

42 Legal writing full time professors program (rather than adjunct professors)

43 Revamped first year courses, and more required focus on history and theoretical concerns.

44 Required foreign, comparative, and international law; reduced requirements for skills

45 More seminars. First year electives.

46 More emphasis on basics and less on vanity courses driven by faculty interests rather than what is in the best interest of the students

76 to 250

1 More substantive law classes.

2 Students should be doing practicums for 1/3 to 1/2 of their second and third years. I understand why Christopher Columbus Langdell introduced the change to the curriculum, but most lawyers today need more practical skills and are not up to the task of being good lawyers. Also, getting rid of US News rankings would free law schools to be more creative in legal education.

3 More clinics and experiential opportunities

4 I would require/offer more interdisciplinary subjects like economics and maybe even some psychology courses, courses that would help learn cultural competency in a meaningful way and I'd require subjects like Constitutional Law II. We have a fairly robust experiential curriculum so I would keep those parts of our curriculum, but I would incorporate more practical/real world aspects into our more doctrinal classes as well.

5 More uniformity in methods & content.

6 Mandatory clinic or practicum

7 Longer (across a year, rather than a semester) first-year courses; more required doctrinal courses

8 Not sure

9 More clinical opportunities
10 More skills and transactional training. Too litigation focused. Much more feedback during the semester.
11 Eliminate all requirements but traditional basic (no distribution requirements), but describe relative value of electives (e.g., bar, practice, seminar). Staff adequately for and specify subject-matter tracks (e.g., environmental, public service, criminal).
12 Smaller classes, more assignments, more student feedback.
13 More clinical and seminar opportunities.
14 Been there; did that. Changes emphasized skills training and experiential learning, while requiring an array of substantive courses linked to areas where our graduates practice most frequently.
15 I would emphasize practical skills more in doctrinal courses, but doing so requires more teaching resources, which are already spread too thin, and thus more state support of the university and law school. Conceptions of practical skills must be transformed, however, to account for the massive societal and environmental changes new lawyers will be facing.
16 I would encourage writing across the curriculum and integrate more drafting in doctrinal classes
17 Provide more professional formation opportunities within the law school building itself
18 I'd go back to more required courses and more 6-hour coursed in the 1L year.
19 Nine
20 No view
21 Elevate legal research, writing, and analytical skills.
22 Thinking like a lawyer rather than learning practice skills which can easily be acquired through externship and mentoring used to be a priority and should be again
23 I would incorporate more writing into each class, teach about AI from the beginning, and start bar prep in the second year.
24 Have the curriculum comprised of fewer required courses and more electives.
25 Less bar focus, more practice focus
26 I would include more practical application in the casebook courses and amplify the legal writing curriculum. I would teach every casebook course like a lab course where legal writing and casebook professors collaborate to provide students with opportunities to work with the concepts they are learning in class. For example, when they are learning about the well-pleaded complaint, maybe their lab has an assignment for them to draft or revise a complaint. Perhaps they critique a complaint. Similar exercises can be created for other courses.
27 Eliminate the !L comp exams
28 More skills development and critical theory
29 Incorporate more education for credit on trauma, trauma-informed lawyering, mental health, and law student/attorney wellbeing
30 More structured
31 Doctrinal courses beyond the first year should integrate more skills.

Other

1 Hire more full time faculty
2 Don't know
3 Hire more faculty for smaller classes and better teaching.
4 More focus on key skills courses, especially courses focusing on basic professionalism and identity skills. More robust expectations for student success.

Table 6.1 How difficult is it at your institution to develop new law courses in emerging or neglected areas?

	No Answer	Very easy	Easy	Neither easy nor difficult	Difficult	Very difficult
Entire sample	1.49%	12.69%	38.81%	32.84%	10.45%	3.73%

Table 6.2 How difficult is it at your institution to develop new law courses in emerging or neglected areas? Broken out by law school enrollment

Law school enrollment	No Answer	Very easy	Easy	Neither easy nor difficult	Difficult	Very difficult
Less than 400	3.13%	6.25%	28.13%	43.75%	12.50%	6.25%
400+ - 550	3.13%	18.75%	34.38%	34.38%	6.25%	3.13%
550+ - 800	0.00%	5.88%	44.12%	29.41%	14.71%	5.88%
More than 800	0.00%	19.44%	47.22%	25.00%	8.33%	0.00%

Table 6.3 How difficult is it at your institution to develop new law courses in emerging or neglected areas? Broken out by academic title

Academic title	No Answer	Very easy	Easy	Neither easy nor difficult	Difficult	Very difficult
Professor	1.64%	16.39%	39.34%	26.23%	13.11%	3.28%
Assistant/ Associate Professor	0.00%	9.52%	28.57%	42.86%	19.05%	0.00%
Adjunct/Clinical Faculty	0.00%	3.57%	32.14%	46.43%	7.14%	10.71%
Emeritus	0.00%	13.33%	73.33%	13.33%	0.00%	0.00%
Other	11.11%	22.22%	22.22%	44.44%	0.00%	0.00%

Table 6.4 How difficult is it at your institution to develop new law courses in emerging or neglected areas? Broken out by age of respondent

Age of respondent	No Answer	Very easy	Easy	Neither easy nor difficult	Difficult	Very difficult
Under 40	0.00%	0.00%	50.00%	33.33%	16.67%	0.00%
40-49	0.00%	26.32%	36.84%	26.32%	10.53%	0.00%
50-59	0.00%	15.15%	27.27%	42.42%	12.12%	3.03%
60 or over	2.67%	9.33%	44.00%	29.33%	9.33%	5.33%
Unknown	0.00%	0.00%	0.00%	100.00%	0.00%	0.00%

Table 6.5 How difficult is it at your institution to develop new law courses in emerging or neglected areas? Broken out by gender of respondent

Gender of respondent	No Answer	Very easy	Easy	Neither easy nor difficult	Difficult	Very difficult
Male	1.25%	12.50%	38.75%	32.50%	8.75%	6.25%
Female	0.00%	14.00%	42.00%	32.00%	12.00%	0.00%
Other	25.00%	0.00%	0.00%	50.00%	25.00%	0.00%

Table 6.6 How difficult is it at your institution to develop new law courses in emerging or neglected areas? Broken out by public or private law school

Public or private law school	No Answer	Very easy	Easy	Neither easy nor difficult	Difficult	Very difficult
Public	1.23%	11.11%	40.74%	33.33%	9.88%	3.70%
Private	1.89%	15.09%	35.85%	32.08%	11.32%	3.77%

Table 6.7 How difficult is it at your institution to develop new law courses in emerging or neglected areas? Broken out by # of courses taught last semester

# of courses taught last semester	No Answer	Very easy	Easy	Neither easy nor difficult	Difficult	Very difficult
None	0.00%	11.11%	51.85%	29.63%	7.41%	0.00%
One	2.50%	12.50%	30.00%	40.00%	12.50%	2.50%
Two	0.00%	13.56%	37.29%	32.20%	11.86%	5.08%
More than two	12.50%	12.50%	50.00%	12.50%	0.00%	12.50%

Table 6.8 How difficult is it at your institution to develop new law courses in emerging or neglected areas? Broken out by ranking

Ranking	No Answer	Very easy	Easy	Neither easy nor difficult	Difficult	Very difficult
Top 20 law school	0.00%	14.81%	33.33%	37.04%	14.81%	0.00%
Somewhere in the 21-75 rank	1.82%	12.73%	43.64%	29.09%	7.27%	5.45%
76 to 250	0.00%	10.87%	34.78%	36.96%	13.04%	4.35%
Other	16.67%	16.67%	50.00%	16.67%	0.00%	0.00%

Table 6.9 How difficult is it at your institution to develop new law courses in emerging or neglected areas? Broken out by political views

Political views	No Answer	Very easy	Easy	Neither easy nor difficult	Difficult	Very difficult
Conservative	0.00%	28.57%	35.71%	21.43%	7.14%	7.14%
Centrist	0.00%	8.82%	38.24%	35.29%	11.76%	5.88%
Liberal	1.54%	9.23%	44.62%	29.23%	13.85%	1.54%
Left of Liberal	5.00%	20.00%	25.00%	45.00%	0.00%	5.00%
Unknown	0.00%	0.00%	0.00%	100.00%	0.00%	0.00%

www.ingramcontent.com/pod-product-compliance
Lightning Source LLC
LaVergne TN
LVHW080527210926
848481LV00022B/3642